# A Note From Rick Renner

I am on a personal quest to see a "revival of the Bible" so people can establish their lives on a firm foundation that will stand strong and endure the test as end-time storm winds begin to intensify.

In order to experience a revival of the Bible in your personal life, it is important to take time each day to read, receive, and apply its truths to your life. James tells us that if we will continue in the perfect law of liberty — refusing to be forgetful hearers, but determined to be doers — we will be blessed in our ways. As you watch or listen to the programs in this series and work through this corresponding study guide, I trust you will search the Scriptures and allow the Holy Spirit to help you hear something new from God's Word that applies specifically to your life. I encourage you to be a doer of the Word He reveals to you. Whatever the cost, I assure you — it will be worth it.

> Thy words were found, and I did eat them;
> and thy word was unto me the joy and rejoicing of mine heart:
> for I am called by thy name, O Lord God of hosts.
> — Jeremiah 15:16

Your brother and friend in Jesus Christ,

*Rick Renner*

Rick Renner

*How To Successfully Divert and Overcome Temptation*

Copyright © 2021 by Rick Renner
P.O. Box 702040
Tulsa, OK 74170

Published by Rick Renner Ministries
www.renner.org

ISBN 13: 978-1-68031-904-0

eBook ISBN 13: 978-1-68031-905-7

# How To Use This Study Guide

This five-lesson study guide corresponds to *"How To Successfully Divert and Overcome Temptation" With Rick Renner* (**Renner TV**). Each lesson in this study guide covers a topic that is addressed during the program series, with questions and references supplied to draw you deeper into your own private study of the Scriptures on this subject.

To derive the most benefit from this study guide, consider the following:

**First,** watch or listen to the program prior to working through the corresponding lesson in this guide. (Programs can also be viewed at **renner.org** by clicking on the Media/Archive links.)

**Second,** take the time to look up the scriptures included in each lesson. Prayerfully consider their application to your own life.

**Third,** use a journal or notebook to make note of your answers to each lesson's Study Questions and Practical Application challenges.

**Fourth,** invest specific time in prayer and in the Word of God to consult with the Holy Spirit. Write down the scriptures or insights He reveals to you.

**Finally,** take action! Whatever the Lord tells you to do according to His Word, do it.

For added insights on this subject, it is recommended that you obtain Rick Renner's books *A Life Ablaze* and *Unlikely — Our Faith-Filled Journey to the Ends of the Earth.* You may also select from Rick's other available resources by placing your order at **renner.org** or by calling 1-800-742-5593.

TOPIC

# Fleeing With Your Feet

## SCRIPTURES

1. **1 Corinthians 10:13** — There hath no temptation taken you but such as is common to man: but God is faithful, who will not suffer you to be tempted above that ye are able; but will with the temptation also make a way to escape, that ye may be able to bear it.

2. **1 Corinthians 10:14** — Wherefore, my dearly beloved, flee from idolatry.

## GREEK WORDS

1. "temptation" — **πειρασμός** (*peirasmos*): an intense examination; a fiery trial or experience

2. "taken" — **λαμβάνω** (*lambano*): to seize; to attack; to grip; to take hold of

3. "common to man" — **ἀνθρώπινος** (*anthropinos*): anything experienced by human beings; unexceptional; merely human

4. "but God is faithful"— **πιστὸς δὲ ὁ Θεός** (*pistos de ho Theos*): but God is categorically faithful

5. "suffer" — **ἐάω** (*eao*): to permit, such as a lurking danger

6. "tempted" — **πειρασμός** (*peirasmos*): an intense examination; a fiery trial or experience

7. "above" — **ὑπὲρ** (*huper*): over, above, beyond; more than; beyond what is normal; something that is excessive

8. "able" — **δύναμαι** (*dunamai*): depicts strength that makes one able, capable, strong, and powerful

9. "with" — **σύν** (*sun*): with; together with; alongside with; accompanying

10. "make" — **ποιέω** (*poieo*): make; creatively make; manufacture or produce; to provide

11. "escape" — **ἔκβασις** (*ekbasis*): to walk out, as to walk out of a difficult place; to walk away; to remove yourself from a person or place that isn't good for you; to use your feet to exit a situation or environment

12. "bear" — ὑποφέρω (*hupophero*): from ὑπό (*hupo*) and φέρω (*phero*); the word ὑπό (*hupo*) means under and the word φέρω (*phero*) means to bear or to carry on; technically, like an undercurrent of a river that sweeps or carries one away; to be carried safely away from danger

13. "flee" — φεύγω (*pheugo*): to run as fast as possible; to escape; to use one's feet to move as fast as possible to get out of an unprofitable situation; picture of one's feet "flying" as he runs from a situation

## SYNOPSIS

The five lessons in this study on *How To Successfully Divert and Overcome Temptation* will focus on the following topics:

- Fleeing With Your Feet
- Fleeing Emotionally Upsetting Temptations
- Fleeing Overeating Temptations
- Fleeing Spending Temptations
- Fleeing Sexual Temptations

**The emphasis of this lesson:**

**God has made a way for you to escape temptation using your own two feet! In fact, He instructs you to *flee* temptation — which means to move your feet as fast as you can and get out of there!**

The ancient city of Smyrna — in the Roman province of Asia — was a massive city filled with pagan temples to worship false gods. One of the oldest temples in the city of Smyrna was the temple of Athena. The Greek world and the Roman world were filled with pagan temples. Believers stayed away from them — and rightfully so — because demon spirits operated in these places. The apostle Paul wrote, "But I say, that the things which the Gentiles sacrifice, they sacrifice to devils, and not to God: and I would not that ye should have fellowship with devils" (1 Corinthians 10:20).

Paul understood that if believers walked into a place where there was an evil spiritual environment, they could become oppressed. He said, "Don't you understand; the statues are nothing, the buildings are nothing, but *in these places demon spirits operate.* This is an environment you don't need to be in!"

Likewise, we need to think about the environments that *we* are in. If you walk into a building where there is an evil spiritual atmosphere, you may walk right in to temptation. Have you ever walked into a place that was spiritually oppressive? Have you spent time with people who were not a good influence? It's always important to think about *where* you are, *what* you're doing, and *what* the spiritual atmosphere is like in the places you go. Stay away from places where you are susceptible to sin or weakness. Use your feet and use your head — be smart!

## You Can Escape Any Type of Temptation

There are all kinds of temptations, and you can successfully divert them or overcome them. "There hath no temptation taken you but such as is common to man: but God is faithful, who will not suffer you to be tempted above that ye are able; but will with the temptation also make a way to escape, that ye may be able to bear it" (1 Corinthians 10:13). Sometimes people get religious with this verse and say, "Well, I know the Lord won't lay on me more than I can bear." My friends, this verse is not describing things that *God* lays on you. These are *attacks*, and we're told in this verse *you can escape any temptation.*

As we examine First Corinthians 10:13, notice Paul says, "There hath no *temptation* taken you but such as is common to man." The word "temptation" is the Greek word *peirasmos*, and it is used three times in this verse, which means it is very important. If you understand the word "temptation," the Greek word *peirasmos*, you know this has nothing to do with what *God* would give you. This word describes *an intense examination,* and *a fiery trial or experience* that usually produces damage or destruction. It depicts something extremely evil that comes to test you, and possibly even destroy you.

First Corinthians 10:13 goes on to describe that no destructive temptation has "taken you." The word "taken" is the Greek word *lambano*, which means *to seize; to attack; to grip;* or *to take hold of.* Have you ever been in a moment when temptation called out to you, and tried to take hold of you? It may have felt like it was seizing you or trying to grip you. It was an attack, and it wasn't sent from God.

## Don't Magnify What Is Tempting You

"There hath no temptation taken you but such as is *common to man*" (1 Corinthians 10:13). No temptation has seized you, attacked you, or tried to lay hold of you but such that is "common to man." The phrase "common to man" is the Greek word *anthropinos*, which is the term for *anything experienced by human beings; unexceptional;* and *merely human.*

If you amplify the thing that is tempting you, it will become bigger in your mind. Rather than glorifying the temptation, look at it and say, "This is *common* to man. There is nothing exceptional about it; I am *not* the first person to encounter this type of temptation. Other people have faced similar situations, and they have overcome. This is *not* a big deal."

The devil wants you to think what you're being tempted by is a big deal. It's *not* a big deal! Don't magnify the temptation. *Diminish it!* Say, "This is small. Millions of people have faced this in the past and they have overcome it, and I'm going to overcome too! There's nothing exceptional about this temptation!" Diminish it! When you diminish temptation, you take the power out of it.

So no temptation has taken you — has tried to seize you, attack you, grip you, or lay hold of you — but that which is common to man, and merely human. But "God is faithful" (1 Corinthians 10:13). The Greek literally says, *pistos de ho Theos.* The word *de* is important because it describes something that is *categorical* or *emphatic.* A better translation would be, "But God is categorically faithful." Never say God has failed you — He has not. God is emphatically faithful!

## With God's Strength, You Are More Than a Match for Any Temptation

Paul continued, "…Who will not *suffer* you to be tempted above that ye are able…" (1 Corinthians 10:13). The word "suffer" is the Greek word *eao*, and means *to permit; such as a lurking danger.* God won't permit you to experience some kind of a prowling danger that's on its way to seize you; He will not *permit* it.

He won't permit you to be "tempted" — the Greek word *peirasmos* — which again describes *an intense examination;* and *a fiery trial or experience.* God will not allow you to be tempted "above" that ye are able. The word "above" is the Greek word *huper*, and it describes something *over, above, beyond; more than; beyond what is normal;* or *something that is excessive.* God won't allow you to experience something that is beyond your ability to control. In fact, First Corinthians 10:13 continues, "…Above that ye are able...." The word "able" — the Greek word *dunamai* — pictures *strength that makes one able, capable, strong, and powerful.*

God has given you everything you need to divert and overcome any kind of temptation that comes your way. With God's strength, you are more than a match for anything that you're dealing with right now. First Corinthians 10:13 goes on to say, "...But will *with* the temptation also make a way to escape, that ye may be able to bear it." The word "with" is the Greek word *sun*, and it means *with; together with; alongside with;* and *accompanying.*

The moment you find yourself confronted with a temptation of any kind, in that moment — immediately — God's grace is there. He is with you, accompanying you, and giving you everything you need to stare it in the face, rebuke it, divert it, and circumvent it. The word "with" means that immediately, in the moment of temptation, God's power is there to partner with you so you can escape!

## Use Your Feet!

How do you find the way of escape from temptation? Most people say, "God! I'm being tempted! Please do something dramatic to get me out of this! Send a bolt of lightning or let someone knock on the door. Make a way for me to escape!" God *has* made a way for you to escape! The word "escape" is the Greek word *ekbasis.* The word *ek* means *out*; the word *basis* means *to walk.* When you compound the two words together to form the word *ekbasis*, it means *to walk out.* It depicts *to walk out of a difficult place; to walk away; to remove yourself from a person or place that isn't good for you; to use your feet to exit a situation or environment.*

God has given you a way of escape — your own two feet. Just like you have walked *into* a bad situation, you can use the same two feet to walk *out* of a situation. God's grace will enable you to walk *away* from it, walk out of it, exit that place, and escape the temptation. Get up! Use your feet and remove yourself from the person or situation that is not good for you!

God has made a way for you to escape, and it's your own feet. You can flee, but you have to use your feet to do it. Get up and walk out. Make an exit from right where you are! Don't stand around and allow yourself to be gripped, attacked, seized, and paralyzed by what you're facing. Use your head and use your feet. Don't believe the lie that you need to stick around and prove how strong you are, because if you do hang around, you'll yield to the temptation. Get up and get out of there! That's what this word *escape* really means.

## Find Yourself Being Tempted? Walk or *Run* Away!

What temptation are you facing? Is it gossip? If you find that you're prone to gossip and you're with a bunch of gossipers — use your feet! Get up and walk out! You don't have to be rude. Just excuse yourself, use your feet, and leave that place. Are you tempted to overeat? Use your feet to get away from that food. You can *walk away* from that temptation.

Are you tempted to become bitter toward others? Remove yourself from that environment. Maybe you're sexually tempted. Use your feet to walk *or run* away from that temptation. Don't stay there and say, "I'm going to prove how strong I am. I'm going to stay here until I can overcome it." If you stay there, you will succumb to it. The Bible never tells you to stay there to prove how strong you are. It admonishes you to use your feet. Get up, and walk away from that situation.

Remember, temptation is common to man. Many, many people have overcome what you're facing, *and you can too*. Do not magnify it. Diminish it! You can conquer anything you're facing because you have the power of the Holy Spirit. Paul admonished, "There hath no temptation taken you but such as is common to man: But God is categorically faithful, who will not allow you to be tempted above that ye are able…." You have the power to overcome it! God will partner with you in the midst of the temptation and make a way to escape: "…That ye may be able to *bear* it" (1 Corinthians 10:13).

The word "bear" is the Greek word *hupophero*, and it is packed with weighty meaning. It is a compound of two words, the word *hupo* meaning *under*, and the word *phero*, indicating *to bear* or *to carry*. When these words are joined to form the word *hupophero*, it means *to be carried under*. It's the picture of *an undercurrent of a river that carries you away*. The grace of God and the power of God will grab you, sweep you out of a dangerous environment, and deliver you to a place of freedom and safety.

## *Flee* From Idolatry

In the very next verse, Paul continues, "Wherefore, my dearly beloved, *flee* from idolatry" (1 Corinthians 10:14). In the First Century, places of idolatry were popular, and a host of temptations were connected with them, such as parties, sexual immorality, drinking, and drugs. Paul didn't say, "Pray to be delivered from that environment." He said, "…Flee from idolatry" (1 Corinthians 10:14). The word "flee" is from the Greek word *pheugo*, which means *to run as fast as possible; to escape;* and *to use one's feet to move as fast as possible to get out of an unprofitable situation.* It pictures *one's feet "flying" as he runs from a situation.*

It is powerful and spiritual *to run.* In fact, run as fast as possible! God never said, "Stay there." He said, "Use your feet! Your feet are your way of escape, so run as fast as your feet can carry you. Escape! Get out of that place!"

## How To Gain Victory over Temptation

In the program, Rick shared:

> Many years ago, back when Denise and I were single adult pastors, a young man came to see me. He kept falling into sexual sin — over and over. One day, I could see by his behavior he was grieved.
>
> Finally, I said to him, "Where does this sexual sin always take place?" He said, "You know, it happens every time I go to my girlfriend's apartment." I said, "Then *maybe you shouldn't go to her apartment.* Stay away from there!" He answered me, "What? You mean you want me to run? You mean run from my weakness? No, I'm going to stay there and prove how strong I am until I overcome this!"
>
> I had already known him for two years, and for two years he had been habitually falling into sin *every time he went to her apartment,* so I said to him, "Your pattern already shows me you're not going to overcome this by staying there. The best thing for you to do is not go there, and if you do go there — use your feet, get up, and get out of there! Use your head!" And my friend, *this applies to all kinds of temptations.*

Maybe you're in an emotionally upsetting situation, and it's a real temptation for you to get bitter in that place. Get out of there! Maybe you're tempted to overeat. What should you do if you are tempted to eat too much? How do you escape that type of temptation? We will deal with that in an upcoming lesson.

You may have an overspending temptation, and know you need to stop using the credit card, but you just can't seem to say, "no." The urge to buy may seem so real. The impulse to have that *next thing* just tugs and tugs on you. How do you overcome? How do you divert the temptation to overspend? Or possibly you struggle with sexual temptation. Maybe you're tempted to look at pornography. How do you overcome that?

All of these temptations are not difficult to overcome, and you need to minimize them. Quit glorifying them; quit magnifying them. Quit looking at yourself like you're a victim, and remember that according to First Corinthians 10:13, God has made you able! And He has provided a way of escape!

In our next lesson, we will begin examining *how* to practically overcome these temptations.

## STUDY QUESTIONS

**Study to shew thyself approved unto God, a workman that needeth not to be ashamed, rightly dividing the word of truth.**
**— 2 Timothy 2:15**

1.  What did Joseph do when he was tempted to commit adultery? Read Genesis 39:7-12. Notice the abruptness of Joseph's response to the persistent initiative of a powerful woman. How would it have impacted Joseph's life if he had not run from temptation? Would he have fulfilled his destiny? What should you do when temptation springs up in your life? How will that impact your future?

2.  "Let no man say when he is tempted, I am tempted of God: for God cannot be tempted with evil, neither tempteth he any man: But every man is tempted, when he is drawn away of his own lust, and enticed. Then when lust hath conceived, it bringeth forth sin: and sin, when it is finished, bringeth forth death" (James 1:13-15). According to this passage, what draws people into temptation? What is the progression or path of temptation described in these verses? What is the end result of yielding to temptation? According to First Corinthians 10:13, how can you divert temptation?

## PRACTICAL APPLICATION

**But be ye doers of the word, and not hearers only, deceiving your own selves.**
**—James 1:22**

1. You have to get very practical about the way you deal with temptation. For example, if pornography is a problem for you — as it is for many men, and even some women — put a filter on your computer and find someone you can be accountable to. What are some practical things you can do to help you divert temptation? (Consider James 4:7; First Peter 2:11; and Second Timothy 2:22.)

2. Don't sit around and allow yourself to become paralyzed by temptation. Don't believe the lie that you need to stick around in order to prove how spiritually strong you are. If you know something is trying to tempt you, get moving before it traps you (*see* 1 Thessalonians 4:1-7). What does First Thessalonians 4:7 say that God has called us to? What action plan can you make to live a holy life? Pour out your heart to the Lord about any temptation you are facing. Realize you are not alone; God is ready to partner with you and help you overcome! Remember, it's your feet that need to get moving away from what is tempting you.

3. Rick mentioned that believers stayed away from pagan temples — and rightfully so because they were loaded with sin and a host of temptations. Write down the names of places you need to stay away from in order to divert temptation. Ask the Holy Spirit to help you consistently stay away from these places. (*See* Proverbs 5:8-13 and Proverbs 4:14-19.)

## LESSON 2

## TOPIC

# Fleeing Emotionally Upsetting Temptations

## SCRIPTURES

1. **1 Corinthians 10:13** — There hath no temptation taken you but such as is common to man: but God is faithful, who will not suffer you to be tempted above that ye are able; but will with the temptation also make a way to escape, that ye may be able to bear it.

2. **1 Corinthians 10:14** — Wherefore, my dearly beloved, flee from idolatry.

3. **Romans 12:18** — If it be possible, as much as lieth in you, live peaceably with all men.

## GREEK WORDS

1. "temptation" — πειρασμός (*peirasmos*): an intense examination; a fiery trial or experience
2. "taken" — λαμβάνω (*lambano*): to seize; to attack; to grip; to take hold of
3. "common to man" — ἀνθρώπινος (*anthropinos*): anything experienced by human beings; unexceptional; merely human
4. "but God is faithful" — πιστὸς δὲ ὁ Θεός (*pistos de ho Theos*): but God is categorically faithful
5. "suffer" — ἐάω (*eao*): to permit, such as a lurking danger
6. "above" — ὑπὲρ (*huper*): over, above, beyond; more than; beyond what is normal; something that is excessive
7. "able" — δύναμαι (*dunamai*): depicts strength that makes one able, capable, strong, and powerful
8. "with" — σύν (*sun*): with; together with; alongside with; accompanying
9. "make" — ποιέω (*poieo*): make; creatively make; manufacture or produce; to provide
10. "escape" — ἔκβασις (*ekbasis*): to walk out, as to walk out of a difficult place; to walk away; to remove yourself from a person or place that isn't good for you; to use your feet to exit a situation or environment
11. "bear" — ὑποφέρω (*hupophero*): from ὑπό (*hupo*) and φέρω (*phero*); the word ὑπό (*hupo*) means under and the word φέρω (*phero*) means to bear or to carry on; technically, like an undercurrent of a river that sweeps or carries one away; to be carried safely away from danger
12. "flee" — φεύγω (*pheugo*): to run as fast as possible; to escape; to use one's feet to move as fast as possible to get out of an unprofitable situation; picture of one's feet "flying" as he runs from a situation
13. "if" — εἰ (*ei*): if; a conditional clause
14. "possible" — δυνατός (*dunatos*): ability; power; amazing ability; to be able, capable, or competent for any task; a force that causes one to be able or capable; competent
15. "as much as lieth in" — ἐξ (*ex*): from, emanating from, as far as it depends on you; as much as it depends on you

16. "live peaceably" — εἰρηνεύοντες (*eireneuontes*): from εἰρηνεύω (*eireneuo*), to cultivate or to keep peace; peace-keeping; harmony-keeping; not strifeful, but peaceful

17. "all men" — πάντων ἀνθρώπων (*panton anthropon*): all, everyone, no one excluded

## SYNOPSIS

The ancient city of Aphrodisias is located in the Roman province of Asia. The reason this city was called Aphrodisias is because it was devoted to the worship of Aphrodite — the goddess of sex. The temple of Aphrodite was the central feature of the city, and beautiful beyond description. Pagans were serious when they built this temple with their stunning craftsmanship, gold, silver, and precious stones. Later, when paganism began to collapse, it was converted into a church.

There were beautiful temples like the temple of Aphrodite all over the Greek world and the Roman world. In First Corinthians 6:19 and 20, Paul said, "What? know ye not that your body is the temple of the Holy Ghost which is in you, which ye have of God, and ye are not your own? For ye are bought with a price: therefore glorify God in your body, and in your spirit, which are God's." The word "temple" is the Greek word *naos,* and it doesn't describe a shack or something made out of mud, straw, and sticks. The word "temple" — *naos* — describes a magnificently built, *highly decorated shrine.* Its marble, granite, gold, silver, and vastly decorated ornamentation combined to create something so marvelous that a god would be happy to live there.

Paul used the word *naos* — the word translated as "temple" — when he said, "Your body is the temple of the Holy Ghost which is in you…" (1 Corinthians 6:19). You're not a mud shack. You're *a magnificent temple.* When the Holy Spirit came to live inside you, He invested *a lot* in you. You may not be filled with gold, silver, and precious stones, but if your eyes were opened to see your interior, you would be quite amazed. You are so magnificent on the inside that God Himself by His Spirit moved into your heart. You really are *the temple of the Holy Spirit.* And that's why First Corinthians 6:20 says, "For ye are bought with a price: therefore glorify God in your body, and in your spirit, which are God's."

The emphasis of this lesson:

You don't have to agree with all people or condone their behavior, but as much as it depends on you — *be at peace with them*. If peace is attainable even in your challenging relationships, give it your best shot. But, if you're being hurt again and again, it may be time to use your feet and remove yourself from the situation.

# A Review of Our Anchor Verse

Our anchor verse for this series declares, "There hath no temptation taken you but such as is common to man: but God is faithful, who will not suffer you to be tempted above that ye are able; but will with the temptation also make a way to escape, that ye may be able to bear it" (1 Corinthians 10:13). The word "temptation" is from the Greek word *peirasmos*, and it is used three times in this verse, which means it is very important.

The word *peirasmos* — or "temptation" — describes *an intense examination, a fiery trial or experience* that comes to burn you up and destroy you. It carries something sinister; that's what a temptation is. Remember, you are the temple of the Holy Spirit. You really *are*! And the devil wants to assault you with temptation to invade you, access you, and tear you down. But you can divert and overcome *every* temptation.

And First Corinthians 10:13 says that there has no temptation "taken" you. The word "taken" is a form of the Greek word *lambano*, which means *to seize; to attack; to grip; or to take hold of.* It describes that moment when some kind of temptation appeals to your flesh, tries to lay hold of you, and attempts to take you into its grip. No temptation has seized you, attacked you, or tried to lay hold of you — but such as is "common to man."

The phrase "common to man" is from the Greek word *anthropinos*, which describes *anything experienced by human beings; unexceptional;* and *merely human.* This is so important because if you glorify the temptation, you give power to it. Rather than magnifying the temptation, diminish it! If you feel something appealing to your flesh, look it in the face and say, "You have no power over me. You're just common to man. Other people have faced you, and they have overcome you. I'm going to overcome you too!"

First Corinthians 10:13 goes on to say, "…But God is faithful…." A better translation would be, "…But God is categorically faithful, who will not allow you to be tempted above and beyond what you're *able* to handle."

The word "able" is a form of the Greek word *dunamai*, which describes *strength that makes one able, capable, strong, and powerful*. God has given you everything you need to deal with *any* temptation. This verse continues, "…But will *with* the temptation…." The word "with" carries the idea of partnership. God will come *alongside* you in the midst of the temptation and provide a way to escape — a way to exit the situation.

## God Will Provide a Way of Escape, But He Needs Your Participation

The word "escape" is the Greek word *ekbasis*, a compound of two words; the word *ek*, which means "out," and the word *basis*, which means "to walk." When you compound the two words together the word "escape" means *to walk out*. A literal translation would be, "God will make a way for you to walk out of that temptation." You don't have to stay there; you can walk away from it. There are some people and places that are not good for you, and you can remove yourself from them. Disconnect from those environments. Use your feet to exit the tempting situations in your life.

The way of escape is in your shoes — it's called *your feet*. Just like you walked *into* a bad situation, you can turn around and walk *out* of it. God will partner Himself with you and give you the power to walk away from the temptation. Paul goes on to say, "…That ye may be able to *bear* it" (1 Corinthians 10:13). The word "bear" — the Greek word *hupophero* — pictures *a current that carries you away from a turbulent situation to a place of safety*. God will carry you from that bad situation and bring you into a place of freedom and deliverance, but He needs *your* participation!

Your feet will move you out of that situation. And that is why Paul immediately follows up and says, "Wherefore, my dearly beloved, flee from idolatry" (1 Corinthians 10:14). He doesn't say, "Pray to be delivered from idolatry." He doesn't instruct, "Stay there and try to overcome it." He says, "Flee!" How do you flee? You use your feet. Some people may say, "Well, I'm just going to stay here and prove how strong I am." That is a stupid thing to do. Use your feet and exit the tempting situation!

The word "flee" in verse 14 is a translation from the Greek word *pheugo*, which means *to run as fast as possible; to escape; to use one's feet to move as fast as possible to get out of an unprofitable situation*. It pictures *one's feet "flying" as you run from a situation*. The Corinthians were surrounded by temples filled with debauchery, drunkenness, sexual promiscuity, drug use, and alcoholism — places of temptation. You can see why they could become tempted if they went into pagan temples. If you find yourself desiring to go into places where you're tempted, use your feet. First of all, don't go there; divert the temptation. Secondly, if you get into a bad situation filled with temptation, use your two feet to walk out of there. Flee! Fleeing from temptation is smart; use your feet and get out of there!

## What To Do When Peace *Is* Attainable in Relationships

There are different kinds of temptations. Emotionally upsetting temptations can be troubling. The Bible instructs us about what to do if a relationship isn't peaceful like it should be. The apostle Paul admonished, "If it be possible, as much as lieth in you, live peaceably with all men" (Romans 12:18). Notice the verse begins by saying, "If it be *possible....*" The very fact that it begins with the word "if" — which is the Greek word *ei* — tells us that there is an open question mark here with no definitive answer. This means there may be times when you will run into a situation where it's not possible to have peace with *all* men.

It can be very difficult to be at peace with some people — not necessarily because *we* are so difficult, but because *they* are so hard to get along with. (Remember, they may think the same of us!) However, regardless of the difficulty of the task or the behavior choices of those we encounter along the way, to the best of our ability, we must give our best efforts to live peaceably with all men.

The word "possible" is the Greek word *dunatos*, which describes *ability; power; amazing ability; to be able, capable, or competent for any task; a force that causes one to be able or capable;* or *competent.* It means God gives us the power to succeed in any situation, but in this verse it denotes the idea of something that is potentially difficult, but nonetheless — *doable.* Because "If it be possible..." begins with the word "if," it casts a shadow on whether or not it is truly doable. This phrase makes it clear that maybe peace *is* attainable — and maybe it *is not.* It could be translated, "*If* it is doable, *if* it is feasible, or *if* it is possible...."

Romans 12:18 continues, "...As much as lieth in you, live peaceably with all men." The entire phrase, "as much as lieth in," is the Greek word *ex*, meaning *from* you, or *emanating from* you. A better translation is, "...As far as it depends on you." God expects us to do our best to live peaceably with all men. "Peaceably" is from the Greek word *eireneuontes*, which means *to cultivate*, or *to keep peace*. Peace has to be cultivated, and peace has to be kept. Once you've finally obtained peace, you must determine that you're going to do your best to make sure it is maintained.

And Romans 12:18 concludes, "If it be possible, as much as lieth in you, live peaceably with *all men*." "All men" means *all* men. The Greek says *panton anthropon*. The word *panton* — translated "all" — is an all-encompassing term that means *everyone* and *excludes no one*. The word *anthropon* — translated "men" — is from the word *anthropos*, which means *all of mankind*, including every male and female of every race, nationality, language, religion, and skin color — no one excluded. The verse does not say we have to *agree* with all men, and it doesn't say we have to *condone the behaviors* of all men. It says, "If it be possible…" we're to be *at peace* with all men.

The following is the Renner Interpretive Version (*RIV*) of Romans 12:18:

**If it's doable at all, as much as it depends on you, and doing everything possible from your side, be at peace with everyone, no one excluded.**

# What To Do When Peace
# *Is Not* Attainable in Relationships

If you're in a situation where peace is *not* attainable, and you're being hurt again, and again, and again — that is *not* good for you. If you're deeply frustrated and angry all the time — every time you're with this particular person, or this group of people — that is *not* healthy. If you're becoming bitter on the inside because of what they *have* or *have not* done, or what they *said* or *didn't* say, then maybe it's time to exit the situation. Removing yourself from that kind of environment may be the wisest thing you can do. Sometimes it's just smarter to *get out of there*.

There is a time for everything, "A time to embrace, and a time to refrain from embracing…" (Ecclesiastes 3:5 *NKJV*). Ecclesiastes 3:7 continues, "A time to keep silence, and a time to speak…." If you're not finding success in a relationship, and you're being hurt again and again — use your brain, *and your feet*, and say, "For some reason, I'm just not able to get along with this person, so I'm going to remove myself from this situation." God will give you different friends!

If you'll walk out of that place, your feet will lead you to someone else who will be a benefit, and you can enjoy positive experiences with them. But you have to use your feet to detach yourself from that negative situation. If you find it's not attainable to be at peace in a relationship, then it's time for you to remove yourself from it and move on. Get into a different environment, and you'll have better experiences in your life.

In our next lesson, we will discover how to divert or overcome the temptation to overeat.

## STUDY QUESTIONS

> Study to shew thyself approved unto God, a workman that needeth
> not to be ashamed, rightly dividing the word of truth.
> — 2 Timothy 2:15

1. Do you want to overcome temptation? *You* have a part to play! Just as simply as you walked *into* a place, you can walk *out* of it. God made the way for you to escape temptation — by using your own two feet to run as fast as you can *away* from it. What portion of First Corinthians 10:13 stands out to you most? How can you apply that to your life?

2. Read John 16:33, First John 4:4, and Romans 8:37. Notice how the Bible calls you an overcomer again and again. Write these three verses out and bolster your faith by reading them during challenging times. The Holy Spirit lives in you, and He is greater than any temptation you may be facing. You have all the strength, all the power, and all the ability you need to overcome *any* temptation.

3. According to God's Word, are there some people that you just shouldn't associate with? Reflect on Proverbs 22:24 and 25. What does the Bible say about making friends with an angry person?

## PRACTICAL APPLICATION

> But be ye doers of the word, and not hearers only,
> deceiving your own selves.
> — James 1:22

1. **When peace *is* attainable in relationships:** Peace needs to be *obtained* and then *maintained* in relationships. Consider Colossians 3:12-14 and First Corinthians 13:4-8 in the *AMPC*. What are some practical

ways you can cultivate peace with others? Write them down and ask the Holy Spirit to help you do them.

2.  **When peace *is not* attainable in relationships:** Do you find yourself in an emotionally upsetting relationship where you've done everything you can from your side, but peace just isn't possible? Why did the Holy Spirit inspire the apostle Paul to begin Romans 12:18 with the word "If..."? Did our loving Heavenly Father know there would be times when peace in a relationship really *wasn't* possible? If you find it's not attainable to be at peace in a relationship, removing yourself from that kind of environment may be the wisest thing you can do. Consider Joshua 1:9; Philippians 4:13; Psalm 18:1,2; and Psalm 138:3.

## LESSON 3

TOPIC

# Fleeing Overeating Temptations

## SCRIPTURES

1.  **1 Corinthians 10:13** — There hath no temptation taken you but such as is common to man: but God is faithful, who will not suffer you to be tempted above that ye are able; but will with the temptation also make a way to escape, that ye may be able to bear it.

2.  **1 Corinthians 10:14** — Wherefore, my dearly beloved, flee from idolatry.

3.  **1 Corinthians 6:19,20** — What? know ye not that your body is the temple of the Holy Ghost which is in you, which ye have of God, and ye are not your own? For ye are bought with a price: therefore glorify God in your body, and in your spirit, which are God's.

4.  **1 Corinthians 10:31** — Whether therefore ye eat, or drink, or whatsoever ye do, do all to the glory of God.

## GREEK WORDS

1.  "temptation" — **πειρασμός** (*peirasmos*): an intense examination; a fiery trial or experience

2. "taken" — λαμβάνω (*lambano*): to seize; to attack; to grip; to take hold of

3. "common to man" — ἀνθρώπινος (*anthropinos*): anything experienced by human beings; unexceptional; merely human

4. "but God is faithful"— πιστὸς δὲ ὁ Θεός (*pistos de ho Theos*): but God is categorically faithful

5. "suffer" — ἐάω (*eao*): to permit, such as a lurking danger

6. "tempted" — πειρασμός (*peirasmos*): an intense examination; a fiery trial or experience

7. "above" — ὑπὲρ (*huper*): over, above, beyond; more than; beyond what is normal; something that is excessive

8. "able" — δύναμαι (*dunamai*): depicts strength that makes one able, capable, strong, and powerful

9. "with" — σύν (*sun*): with; together with; alongside with; accompanying

10. "make" — ποιέω (*poieo*): make; creatively make; manufacture or produce; to provide

11. "escape" — ἔκβασις (*ekbasis*): to walk out, as to walk out of a difficult place; to walk away; to remove yourself from a person or place that isn't good for you; to use your feet to exit a situation or environment

12. "bear" — ὑποφέρω (*hupophero*): from ὑπό (*hupo*) and φέρω (*phero*); the word ὑπό (*hupo*) means under and the word φέρω (*phero*) means to bear or to carry on; technically, like an undercurrent of a river that sweeps or carries one away; to be carried safely away from danger

13. "flee" — φεύγω (*pheugo*): to run as fast as possible; to escape; to use one's feet to move as fast as possible to get out of an unprofitable situation; picture of one's feet "flying" as he runs from a situation

14. "body" — σῶμα (*soma*): the physical body

15. "temple" — ναός (*naos*): a temple or a highly decorated shrine; the image of vaulted ceilings, marble, granite, gold, silver, and highly decorated ornamentation; used in the Old Testament Septuagint to describe the most sacred, innermost part of a temple; the Holy of Holies

16. "glorify" — δοξάζω (*doxadzo*): from δοκέω (*dokeo*): to think or to estimate; honor; value; to show weight and worth

17. "lasciviousness"— ἀσέλγεια (*aselgeia*): excess; primarily refers to the excessive consumption of food or wild, undisciplined living that is especially marked by unbridled sex

# SYNOPSIS

The ruins of the ancient city of Aphrodisias are located in the Roman province of Asia. The name Aphrodisias was acquired because the whole city was dedicated to the worship of Aphrodite, who was the Greek goddess of sex. The great temple of Aphrodite — in the city of Aphrodisias — was quite amazing, and when the pagans built this massive temple, they invested *a lot* into it. It took a great deal of money to construct a temple like this, and had you walked into it during the First Century when the church was first being established in this city, you would have been amazed at the gold, silver, precious stones, and ornamentation that filled this structure.

Temples like the temple of Aphrodite were scattered all over the Greek world and the Roman world. They are what Paul had in mind when he wrote, "Know ye not that ye are the temple of God, and that the Spirit of God dwelleth in you?" (1 Corinthians 3:16). The Greek word *naos* — translated as "temple" — of Aphrodite was the *dwelling place* of Aphrodite. That is the same word Paul used in First Corinthians 3:16, but he used it to say, "We are the *naos* — the temple — of the Holy Spirit." Just like the pagans invested a lot in their physical temples, *God* invested a lot in you! What a boost for your self-image! God provided the blood of Jesus, and then He put the gifts of the Spirit and the fruit of the Spirit in you.

If our eyes were opened and we could really see our spiritual interiors, we would be *amazed*. God has invested a spiritual fortune in us! We are the *naos* — the temple of God, and the Holy Spirit dwells in us. There's much more than meets the eye inside each of us. We are *the temple* of the Holy Spirit.

**The emphasis of this lesson:**

**The temptation to overeat can be self-sabotaging and undercut your confidence due to weight gain, embarrassment, and self-disappointment. The vicious cycle of losing weight and gaining it back can leave you discouraged. This lesson is aimed to inspire you to break the cycle and replace old habits with a new approach. You can also gain powerful revelation that your body really is the temple of the Holy Spirit, and you are so valuable to God that you were bought with the precious blood of Jesus. "Whether therefore ye eat, or drink, or whatsoever ye do, do all to the glory of God" (1 Corinthians 10:31).**

# A Summary of Our Anchor Verse

Most temptations can be diverted, but if you find that you're already in one, you can overcome it. Regardless of how educated, uneducated, rich, or poor you are, know that we all deal with things that come to assail us and tempt us. And we need to know how to divert and overcome them.

In First Corinthians 10:13, the apostle Paul wrote, "There hath no temptation taken you but such as is common to man: but God is faithful, who will not suffer you to be tempted above that ye are able; but will with the temptation also make a way to escape, that ye may be able to bear it." The word "temptation" — the Greek word *peirasmos* — carries the idea of something *fiery* and *intense* that comes to destroy. Everything about this word is negative. Temptation is not something sent by the Lord; it is sent by the enemy or the flesh, and it comes to destroy.

But this verse also says that no temptation "has *taken* you." The word "taken" is a form of the Greek word *lambano,* which means *to seize*; *to attack*; *to grip*; and *to lay hold of.* It depicts that moment when a temptation reaches out to grab hold of your emotions or your flesh and tries to seize you and drag you into an act you should not carry out.

And it also instructs us that there is no temptation "but such as is *common to man.*" The phrase "common to man" is a translation from the Greek word *anthropinos* — and it means *anything experienced by human beings.* It depicts something *unexceptional;* and *merely human.* So when you feel your flesh or a temptation trying to reach out and grab hold of you, rather than saying, "This is so powerful, I can't resist it," simply *minimize* it! Look at it and say, "You are nothing exceptional; you're common to man. Other people have overcome you, and I will overcome you too!" Don't amplify the temptation. If you magnify it, you give power to it. Minimize it!

The apostle Paul continued, "…But God is faithful…" (1 Corinthians 10:13). You could translate this, "But God is categorically faithful." He is not abandoning you; He is not leaving you to deal with this by yourself. God is emphatically *faithful.* Paul continued, "…Who will not suffer you to be tempted above that ye are able." The word "tempted" — again the Greek word *peirasmos* — describes something that has come to destroy, injure, and take you down. And the word "able" — the Greek word *dunamai* — carries the idea of strength that makes one *capable; strong;* and *powerful*. God has given you everything you need — right inside you — to divert or to overcome this temptation.

# How To Escape Temptation

First Corinthians 10:13 goes on to say, "…But will with the temptation also make a way to escape…." The word "with" is the Greek word *sun* which pictures *together with; alongside with;* and *accompanying*. It carries the idea of partnership, which means our faithful God will join Himself with you in the midst of the temptation, and "make a way to escape." The word "make" is a form of the Greek word *poieo*, which means *to make; to creatively make; to manufacture or produce;* and *to provide*. God will creatively provide a way for you to escape the thing that is assailing you!

The word "escape," as we've seen in previous lessons, is the Greek word *ekbasis* — a compound word from the Greek words *ek* and *basis*. The word *ek* means *out*, and it's where we get the word "exit." The word *basis* means *to step*. So when compounded, the word *ekbasis* — translated "escape" — means *to walk out; to walk out of a difficult place; to remove yourself from a person or place that isn't good for you; to use your feet to exit a situation or an environment.*

When you cry out, "God, please make a way for me to escape this temptation," God answers you by saying, "I'm joining you right now to help you do what you need to do, and you need to use your feet. Get up and get out of there!" If you're tempted by pornography, get away from it! If you're tempted to stay in troubled relationships, get out of there! If you're tempted to overspend, leave that place, and make an exit!

Paul goes on to say, "…That you may be able to *bear* it" (1 Corinthians 10:13). The word "bear" is the Greek word *hupophero*; the word *hupo* means *under*, and the word *phero* means *to bear;* or *to carry*. When you compound the two words together, it describes *the undercurrent of a river that picks you up and carries you safely away from danger.* The grace of God will grab hold of you, remove you out of that turbulent situation, and deliver you to the shores safely separated from the temptation. God says there's a way of "escape" — *ekbasis* — and it's *your feet*. Get up and get out of there!

# 'Flee from Idolatry'

The very next verse says, "Wherefore, my dearly beloved, flee from idolatry" (1 Corinthians 10:14).

When we hear the word "idolatry" we may not understand it, but in the First Century, idolatry was associated with sex outside of marriage, drunkenness, drug use, and all kinds of temptations.

People went to the temples where these acts of idolatry were taking place. And Paul was writing to Corinthians who were given to these kinds of things. He said, "If you want to be delivered, here's how: Use your feet. Flee! Get out of there!" The word "flee" in Greek means *to run as fast as possible; to escape; to use one's feet to move as fast as possible to get out of an unprofitable situation.* It pictures one's feet "flying" as he runs from a situation.

We saw in our last lesson that if you are in a troubled relationship and you're constantly being hurt, or you find yourself becoming bitter, it may be time to remove yourself from the relationship. Romans 12:18 says, "*If it be possible, as much as lieth in you, live peaceably with all men.*" "If" indicates that sometimes it's *not* possible to live peaceably with all men. If you find yourself in a relationship where every time you're with that person, you're hurt, troubled, or disturbed — use your feet and remove yourself from that environment.

In future lessons, we will discuss the temptation to overspend, and sexual temptation. In this lesson, we will learn how to overcome overeating.

## How To Divert and Overcome the Temptation To Overeat

In the program, Rick shared:

> "My friend, I have no judgment for you if overeating is a temptation you face. I lost 100 pounds because I had to overcome an overeating temptation. When you're overweight and you overeat, you deal with excess weight, and feel bad about it. You have health issues, which are caused by the fact that you've been overeating and not taking care of your body. You're embarrassed to see others because when others see you, they will see you've gained weight. You have a lot of self-anger because you're mad at yourself for what you've done.
>
> "There's self-disappointment and covering yourself up with clothes — *layers and layers* of clothes — and wearing lots of black, trying to hide the excess pounds. You lose weight, and gain

weight, then lose weight, and gain weight. You spend a lot of money on diets that you're unfaithful to follow through on. My friend, that's not what God wants for you! It certainly is not what God wanted for *me*! I had to make a decision to do something to divert this temptation and to overcome it.

"What really helped me was First Corinthians 6:19 and 20 which says, 'What? know ye not that your body is the temple of the Holy Ghost which is in you, which ye have of God, and ye are not your own? For ye are bought with a price: therefore glorify God in your body, and in your spirit, which are God's.'"

The word "body" in First Corinthians 6:19 is the Greek word *soma*, and it refers to *the physical body*. Paul said, "Your physical body, the one that you're sitting in right now, is the temple of the Holy Ghost." The word "temple" is the Greek word *naos*, and it describes *a temple*; or *a highly decorated shrine*. It's the image of *vaulted ceilings, marble, granite, gold, silver,* and *highly decorated ornamentation*. It's the same word used in the Old Testament Septuagint to describe the most sacred, innermost part of a temple: The Holy of Holies.

This means *God moved inside you* — He *lives* in your physical body. Your body is a walking sanctuary. If your eyes were opened to see what was *inside you*, it would impact the way you treat your body. We would all treat our bodies better if we understood what a sacred place we really are.

First Corinthians 6:20 is clear in its instruction and exhortation: "For ye are bought with a price: therefore glorify God in your body, and in your spirit, which are God's." The word "glorify" is a form of the Greek word *dokeo*, which means *to think*; *to estimate*; *to show weight and worth*; *to honor*; and *to value*. It means you need to put a lot of thought into what you're doing with your body because your body was purchased with the blood of Jesus. You need to carefully consider how to glorify God in your body.

## 'Do All to The Glory of God'

In the program, Rick continued:

"Here is a verse that really confronted me: 'Whether therefore ye eat, or drink, or whatsoever ye do, do all to the glory of God' (1 Corinthians 10:31). Notice that of all the things Paul could have talked about, he said, 'Whether therefore, ye eat, or drink....'

He drew attention to what we are eating, and what we are drinking. He said, 'Do all to the glory of God.' And here we have a very simple test: *Can you eat what you're eating to the glory of God? Can you eat the quantities you're eating to the glory of God? Can you eat junk food to the glory of God? Can you be a glutton to the glory of God?* Of course, the answer is 'no.'"

Galatians 5:19 says, "Now the works of the flesh are manifest, which are these; Adultery, fornication uncleanness, *lasciviousness.*" It mentions one of the works of the flesh as "lasciviousness." That is an old King James word — the Greek word *aselgeia* — and it describes *excess;* or *anything that is in excess.* It primarily refers to *the excessive consumption of food or wild undisciplined living that is especially marked by unbridled sex.* What's amazing is that the word "lasciviousness" — from the Greek word *aselgeia* — is the very word used in Second Peter 2:7 to describe the principal sin of Sodom and Gomorrah. Those were cities of perversion — *lasciviousness.* Therefore, we can see that overeating, in the mind of God, is just as perverted as perverse sexual activities.

You may ask, "Why would excessive or undisciplined eating be considered *that* perverted?" And the answer is because *it destroys the human body.* Your body is made in the image of God. If you're a born-again believer, you are the temple of the Holy Spirit, and these activities corrupt the temple of God. The flesh in its fallen state has one aim: Destruction. Don't let your flesh have its own way.

## How To Bring Change to Your Eating Habits

In the program, Rick concluded:

"You need a plan to bring a change to your life. I had a plan, but *first of all* I had to recognize what I was doing was wrong. I decided to honor my body as the temple of the Holy Spirit, and I lost 100 pounds. Do you know how I did it? I walked out of some situations. I asked my family and my friends to help me be accountable to make sure I was surrounded by the right things, and not by the wrong things. And if I was going to eat something that wasn't good for me, I authorized them to tell me 'no.'

"They helped me divert the temptation, and in the process, I overcame it and I found victory! And, my friend, you can too! You can walk away from the table. You can walk away from eating too much. God has given you a mind to make choices; and He has given you feet to enable you to walk out. Know that *He will be with you in the temptation*, which means you're not facing that plate of food by yourself! He is with you, empowering you to do the right thing, but you are the only one who can make the choice to get up and walk away from it.

"My friend, we're told to glorify God in our bodies. Can you glorify God in the way you're treating yourself right now? Can you glorify God in the way you're eating? If the answer is 'no,' then it's time for you to take action, and walk away from what you've been doing. You *can* divert that temptation, or you *can* overcome it."

## STUDY QUESTIONS

**Study to shew thyself approved unto God, a workman that needeth not to be ashamed, rightly dividing the word of truth.**
**— 2 Timothy 2:15**

1. Read Romans 8:1. There is no condemnation for your actions of the past. Today is a new day, and with the help of the Holy Spirit and the right plan, you can divert or overcome overeating. Ask the Holy Spirit to help you find the right plan of action to lose weight. Say the following scripture several times and write it out on a note card so it is ready to pull out if you need it! "I keep under my body, and bring it into subjection..." (1 Corinthians 9:27).

2. In the program, Rick candidly shared his journey to victory over eating too much, and how he lost 100 pounds. He stated, "You need a plan to bring a change to your life. I had a plan, but first of all — I had to recognize what I was doing was wrong." Take a moment to honestly reflect on your eating habits (*see* Psalm 51:6).

   • Can you eat what you're eating and the quantities you're eating to the glory of God?

   • Can you eat junk food to the glory of God?

   • How can you use your feet to overcome the temptation to overeat?

## PRACTICAL APPLICATION

> But be ye doers of the word, and not hearers only,
> deceiving your own selves.
> —James 1:22

1. "The Lord knoweth how to deliver the godly out of temptations…" (2 Peter 2:9). Trust God to show you *how* to overcome this temptation. See Him partnering with you every step of the way. Ask the Holy Spirit to lead you to the practical knowledge you need to lose weight. He will help you discover the best plan for your victory!

2. Rick authorized his friends and family to hold him accountable for his eating. He said, "They helped me divert the temptation [to overeat], and in the process I overcame it, and I found victory!" Who will you authorize to hold you accountable for your eating? Are you willing to ask them to say, "no" to you when you are making a poor eating choice? "Two are better than one…" (Ecclesiastes 4:9). You are not alone in the journey. Take a moment to pour out your heart to Him and ask the Holy Spirit for His help.

3. Do you want to lose weight? You can do it! Write down how much you want to lose. Now, get very practical about dealing with the temptation to overeat. Ask yourself:

   • What time of day is the temptation to overeat most pronounced? What activity can I plan during that time to keep me focused elsewhere?

   • What food is it that I usually end up overeating? Can I keep that particular food out of reach? What healthy food can I replace it with?

   • Am I willing to end eating habits that need to end, and embrace a new beginning?

## TOPIC
# Fleeing Spending Temptations

## SCRIPTURES

1. **1 Corinthians 10:13** — There hath no temptation taken you but such as is common to man: but God is faithful, who will not suffer you to be tempted above that ye are able; but will with the temptation also make a way to escape, that ye may be able to bear it.

2. **1 Corinthians 10:14** — Wherefore, my dearly beloved, flee from idolatry.

3. **1 John 5:21** — Little children, keep yourselves from idols. Amen.

4. **2 Timothy 3:3** — Without natural affection, trucebreakers, false accusers, incontinent, fierce, despisers of those that are good.

## GREEK WORDS

1. "temptation" — **πειρασμός** (*peirasmos*): an intense examination; a fiery trial or experience

2. "taken" — **λαμβάνω** (*lambano*): to seize; to attack; to grip; to take hold of

3. "common to man" — **ἀνθρώπινος** (*anthropinos*): anything experienced by human beings; unexceptional; merely human

4. "but God is faithful" — **πιστὸς δὲ ὁ Θεός** (*pistos de ho Theos*): but God is categorically faithful

5. "suffer" — **ἐάω** (*eao*): to permit, such as a lurking danger

6. "tempted" — **πειρασμός** (*peirasmos*): an intense examination; a fiery trial or experience

7. "above" — **ὑπὲρ** (*huper*): over, above, beyond; more than; beyond what is normal; something that is excessive

8. "able" — **δύναμαι** (*dunamai*): depicts strength that makes one able, capable, strong, and powerful

9. "with" — **σύν** (*sun*): with; together with; alongside with; accompanying

10. "make" — **ποιέω** (*poieo*): make; creatively make; manufacture or produce; to provide

11. "escape" — ἔκβασις (*ekbasis*): to walk out, as to walk out of a difficult place; to walk away; to remove yourself from a person or place that isn't good for you; to use your feet to exit a situation or environment

12. "bear" — ὑποφέρω (*hupophero*): from ὑπό (*hupo*) and φέρω (*phero*); the word ὑπό (*hupo*) means under and the word φέρω (*phero*) means to bear or to carry on; technically, like an undercurrent of a river that sweeps or carries one away; to be carried safely away from danger

13. "flee" — φεύγω (*pheugo*): to run as fast as possible; to escape; to use one's feet to move as fast as possible to get out of an unprofitable situation; picture of one's feet "flying" as he runs from a situation

14. "keep" — φυλάσσω (*phulasso*): to save, protect, preserve, or to guard; depicted the uninterrupted vigilance shepherds showed in keeping their flocks; used to depict a military guard who exercised unbroken vigilance; guard, protect, secure, shield, or watch over in order to protect one from some outside foul force

15. "from" — ἀπό (*apo*): from; away from; implies intentional distance

16. "idols" — εἴδωλον (*eidolon*): plural, idols or false gods

17. "amen" — ἀμήν (*amen*): amen; so let it be; an emphasis marker used to emphasize a statement of great importance

18. "incontinent" — ἀκρατής (*akrates*): derived from the word κράτος (*kratos*), one of many Greek words that depicts power; but when an *a* is added to the front of it, that has a canceling effect; rather than picturing power, the word shifts to picture a person or society who has lost power over self and therefore has no self-control; refers to the inability to exercise control, a lack of control, a lack of self-restraint, no will power, or the inability to say, "no"

## SYNOPSIS

There are remains of a bouleuterion located in the upper part of ancient Ephesus. The bouleuterion was the place the city council regularly met to discuss laws, and devise solutions to society's severe problems. Two thousand years later, we're still talking about the problems of society, but *we're* living in the last days. The Bible clearly promises that at the very end of the age — the time we're living in right now — the ills of society will be *more severe* than ever before.

In Second Timothy 3:3, the Holy Spirit describes the characteristics of an end-time society. And in First Timothy and Second Timothy, the apostle

Paul gave us solid advice about how to carry out end-time ministry. He particularly spoke to people in the church who will be living at the end of the age — Paul was talking about *us*. He told us what we have to do to effectively minister to people who are impacted by an end-time society. There is confusion on *every* level, and it's an indication of the end of the age. People don't know what is right and wrong. They're even confused about their gender.

**The emphasis of this lesson:**

**In today's society, countless people fall into the trap of overspending. Many live with no boundaries financially, don't know how to say "no," and use credit cards to overspend. The lack of self-restraint is abundant. But God's plan for you is financial freedom, and if you will use your feet to flee the temptation to overspend and use your head to budget persistently and live within your means, you can enjoy financial freedom!**

# A Review of First Corinthians 10:13

"There hath no temptation taken you but such as is common to man: but God is faithful, who will not suffer you to be tempted above that ye are able; but will with the temptation also make a way to escape, that ye may be able to bear it" (1 Corinthians 10:13). The word "temptation" — the Greek word *peirasmos* — is used three times in this verse, and all three times it describes *an intense examination; a fiery trial or experience* that comes to attack you. Temptations come to seduce, harm, and destroy you.

We've seen that the word "taken" is a form of the Greek word *lambano*, which means *to seize; to attack; to grip;* and *to take hold of.* Here it describes the lure of temptation to reach out to our flesh, grab hold of us, and seduce us into doing something we ought not to do. There has no temptation taken you but such as is "common to man" — the Greek word *anthropinos*, describes *anything experienced by all human beings; merely human; unexceptional.*

It is vital that you do not glorify temptation. If you magnify it, you empower it. Instead, diminish it and downsize it! Take the power out of it by saying, "I'm going to overcome you because there's nothing exceptional about you. You're common to man." First Corinthians 10:13 continues by saying, God is "faithful" — meaning, "God is categorically faithful." He will not permit you to be tempted above what you are "able." The word "able" is a form of the Greek word *dunamai*, and it carries the idea of *strength that makes one able, capable, strong, and powerful*. You are capable of dealing with what is trying to assail you. God has given you everything you need to divert it or to overcome it.

First Corinthians 10:13 goes on to say, "…But will with the temptation also make a way to escape…." The word "with" — the Greek word *sun* — carries the idea of partnership. When you're facing something that is tempting your flesh, God Himself — who is faithful — comes alongside you as your partner and makes a way to escape.

## Your 'Flying' Feet Can Carry You to Freedom

Notice the word "escape" — the Greek word *ekbasis*, which means *to walk out of a bad situation; to remove yourself from a person or place that isn't good for you; to use your feet to exit a situation or an environment*. The way of escape is in your shoes, and it's called *your feet*. You may have walked *into* something bad, and you can turn around and walk *out* of it.

God has given you feet, and those feet can carry you to your freedom; you just need to use your brain and use your feet. Say, "I'm going to embrace the grace of God! He is with me in this; He's partnering with me and giving me the power to do what is right. I'm going to turn around and walk out of this."

First Corinthians 10:13 concludes, "…That ye may be able to *bear* it." The word "bear" describes *an undercurrent that picks you up and takes you somewhere else*. God will grab hold of you and carry you out of that turbulent place and deliver you to the banks of safety. But you have to embrace the grace; you have to make the choice, and you have to decide to walk out of it.

Paul continued with, "Wherefore, my dearly beloved, flee from idolatry" (1 Corinthians 10:14). He didn't say, "Stay there and prove you can overcome it; stay there and be strong." He said, "Flee!" The Greek word for "flee" means *to run as fast as possible*. Running is smart. Use your feet to move as fast as possible to get out of an unprofitable situation. The Greek word literally pictures one's feet *flying* as you *run* from a situation.

# Put as Much Space as Possible
# Between Yourself and Temptation

In First John 5:21, the apostle John wrote about fleeing idolatry. Pagan temples were places filled with idolatry and temptations such as sexual promiscuity, alcoholism, drug abuse, and more. The Early New Testament believers spent time in those corrupt places *before* they came to Christ. Though they were delivered, they still felt the lure to go back into those places. First John 5:21 admonishes, "Little children, *keep* yourselves from idols. Amen."

The word "keep" is very intentional. It is the Greek word *phulasso*, which means *save*. It could be translated *to save, to protect, to preserve*, or *to guard*. It depicts *the uninterrupted vigilance shepherds showed in keeping their flocks from wolves*. It was used to portray *a military guard who exercised unbroken vigilance*; and to *guard, protect, secure, shield, or watch over in order to protect one from some outside foul force*. John was saying, "Protect yourself, preserve yourself, and guard yourself from idols." This kind of "keeping" is intentional. You have to make a decision to protect yourself.

John goes on to say we are to "keep ourselves *from* idols. Amen." The word "from" in Greek is the word *apo*, and it carries the idea of *intentional distance*. John is admonishing readers to create intentional distance from all the temptations connected with idolatry. He ends First John 5:21 with the word "Amen" which means *amen; so let it be*. It is used *to emphasize a statement of great importance*.

The following is the *Renner Interpretive Version* (*RIV*) of First John 5:21:

> **Little children, I immediately order you to withdraw from idols. Those idols — and what they represent — are so evil that you need to seriously guard yourself against them and stay away from them altogether. I'm leaving no wiggle room on this issue. I'm absolutely and emphatically ordering you to immediately put as much space as possible between yourself and idols. They are evil and represent a menace to your life, so you must urgently guard against them. What I'm telling you right now is not open for debate and is not optional. It is an order that I fully expect you to obey. In fact, to underscore the seriousness of what I am telling you, I'm even adding an "amen" to stress**

the point. I expect you to explicitly obey my instructions on this issue — and do it now!

# You Can Divert or Overcome the Temptation To Overspend

Do you live on credit, spend what you don't have, and buy what you don't need? Are you driven to purchase, purchase, purchase, and then live with self-anger for what you've done? My friend, this does not have to be your way of life. The Holy Spirit told us this would be indicative of society at the end of the age. (Note: Rick's book *Last Days Survival Guide* covers all the symptoms the Holy Spirit prophesied would transpire in society at the end of the age — the age we're living in.)

Second Timothy 3:3 says people will be "…Without natural affection, trucebreakers, false accusers, *incontinent*, fierce, despisers of those that are good." The word "incontinent" has to do with living in debt. It is the Greek word *akrates* — a compound of the word *kratos* and the word *a*. The word *kratos* is one of many Greek words that *depicts power*, but an *a* added to the front of it has *a canceling effect*. Rather than picturing power, the word shifts to picture *a person or society who has lost power over self and therefore has no self-control*. It refers to *the inability to exercise control, a lack of control, a lack of self-restraint, no will power*, or *the inability to say "no."* It pictures one who has lost power, one who has lost self-control, and therefore has no mastery over himself. It depicts society at the end of the age saying "yes" to everything they want to buy (whether they can afford it or not).

The Holy Spirit prophesied this would be indicative of people at the end of the age. Obvious symptoms of an end-time society include the fact that people are self-focused, self-absorbed, and self-centered. And the truth is the lack of self-restraint is abundant in society today. Many people are living with no boundaries, don't know how to say "no," and use credit cards to overspend.

The word "incontinent" indicates people will buy *what* they want, *when* they want it — with no regard for its value, and no patience to wait for it. It describes people who accrue debt to get what they don't even need because they are self-absorbed and can't say "no." They are covetous and want it *now*, so they buy it whether they can afford it or not.

# The Trap of Excess Living, Exorbitant Spending, and Mindless Consumerism

When people overspend, they end up as slaves to debt. This is not the will of God for your life! The Holy Spirit prophesied that people at the end of the age would be hurled into excessive living, outrageous spending, and mindless consumerism. Have you fallen into the trap of overspending? *Anyone* can fall into it. The facts show that Americans today are making more money than ever before yet feel they have less than ever because they're using their money to pay off debt and living in slavery to their past actions!

If this is your current situation, it doesn't have to be a life sentence. Listen to the Holy Spirit, do what is right, and you can reverse this condition. Remember, the word "escape" means *to walk out.* Just like you walked *into* the mess you're in, you can turn around and walk *out* of it. You may not get out of debt immediately, but you can begin taking steps in the right direction. Rather than living with this sentence over your life, you can change the way you're living, cut up your credit cards, and put boundaries on your spending. Faithfully give your tithes and offerings, budget persistently, and believe God will bless the work you put your hand to — and He will!

My friend, you have to embrace the grace of God to step out of the trap of overspending. Avoid the temptation to buy things you don't need. If you're headed somewhere you know you'll be tempted to overspend, make the decision to divert from that place. Don't go there, and you will avoid getting into more debt. According to First Corinthians 10:13, God will join Himself with you so you don't have to face the struggle by yourself, and He will make a way for the current of His Grace to grab you, pull you out of a turbulent place, and deliver you on the banks of safety and security. That is the plan of God for your life! But it requires *your* mind, *your* decisions, and *your* actions.

You have the ability to flee the temptation to overspend! We've already seen in First John 5:21 that you need to intentionally put space between you and the thing that's calling out to your flesh. Put space between yourself and excessive spending so you don't fall victim to it, and you will *become* free and *stay* free. Then, when God tugs on your heart to give, you can joyfully sow into every good work.

# You Can Walk in Financial Freedom

You *can* do the right thing when it comes to your spending. You *can* stop falling victim to the spirit of the age which says, "Buy, buy, buy. Charge, charge, charge...." Put distance between yourself and excessive spending; stop buying things that cause you to say later, "Why did I buy this? I don't even need it! I don't even use it!" Why put yourself in slavery to debt? Put distance between yourself and temptations to overspend.

We're living in the end of the age when people are "incontinent" — the Greek word *akrates* — meaning people are not living wisely but over-spending and ending up slaves to debt. That doesn't have to be you! The Holy Spirit said it will happen to people on a wide scale at the end of the age, but God's plan for you is financial freedom, and you can walk in it!

## STUDY QUESTIONS

**Study to shew thyself approved unto God, a workman that needeth not to be ashamed, rightly dividing the word of truth.**
**— 2 Timothy 2:15**

"Beloved, I wish above all things that thou mayest prosper and be in health, even as thy soul prospereth" (3 John 2).

1. The Scriptures tell us, "Godliness with contentment is great gain" (1 Timothy 6:6). What does Philippians 4:11-13 instruct us to do? If you have overspent in the past, what type of freedom can you enjoy by obeying these two verses? Meditate on the truth in these verses, and you will be transformed by the renewing of your mind in the area of contentment (*see* Romans 12:2).

2. What can we learn from First Timothy 6:7 when it comes to our perspective on earthly things? According to First Timothy 6:8, having food and clothing, what are we instructed to do?

3. According to Colossians 3:1-3, where are we to set our affections? Why are we instructed to set our affections there? How can gaining this perspective help you divert or overcome the temptation to over-spend?

4. Thankfully, the temptation to overspend can be diverted, but if you're already in debt, *you can overcome it.* "Ye are of God, little children, and have overcome them: because greater is he that is in you, than he that

is in the world" (1 John 4:4). The One who is in you *is greater* than the temptation to overspend. (Consider First Corinthians 15:57.)

## PRACTICAL APPLICATION

**But be ye doers of the word, and not hearers only,
deceiving your own selves.
— James 1:22**

1. God does not want you to be a slave to debt. You can turn around, break the cycle of overspending, and walk out of debt. Ask the Holy Spirit for wisdom and practical steps to freedom. Read James 1:5, Proverbs 19:8, and Proverbs 24:3 and 4. Write down the steps He gives you and hold yourself accountable to do them! Remember, it took time to walk *into* the financial situation you are in, and it will take time to walk *out* of it.

2. Write down the places you need to stay away from in order to protect yourself from the temptation to overspend. Ask a friend or family member to hold you accountable to stay away from those locations.

3. Advertisements say things like, "Buy now; buy now!" If you're not careful, you will fall victim to the spirit of the age. The "debt trap" that awaits has steep consequences and will hinder your lifestyle in the future if you fall into it! Renew your mind to the truth about stewarding your finances, and choose to live within your means. (Consider also Proverbs 18:15, Psalm 23:1-3, and First Timothy 6:10 and 11.)

## LESSON 5

## TOPIC

# Fleeing Sexual Temptations

## SCRIPTURES

1. **1 Corinthians 10:13** — There hath no temptation taken you but such as is common to man: but God is faithful, who will not suffer you to be tempted above that ye are able; but will with the temptation also make a way to escape, that ye may be able to bear it.

2. **1 Corinthians 10:14** — Wherefore, my dearly beloved, flee from idolatry.

3. **2 Timothy 2:22** — Flee also youthful lusts....

4. **1 Thessalonians 4:4** — That every one of you should know how to possess his vessel in sanctification and honour.

5. **Romans 13:14** (*ESV*) — But put on the Lord Jesus Christ, and make no provision for the flesh, to gratify its desires.

6. **Hebrews 13:4** (*ESV*) — Let marriage be held in honor among all, and let the marriage bed be undefiled, for God will judge the sexually immoral and adulterous.

7. **Galatians 6:1** — Brethren, if a man be overtaken in a fault, ye which are spiritual, restore such an one in the spirit of meekness; considering thyself, lest thou also be tempted.

## GREEK WORDS

1. "temptation" — **πειρασμός** (*peirasmos*): an intense examination; a fiery trial or experience

2. "taken" — **λαμβάνω** (*lambano*): to seize; to attack; to grip; to take hold of

3. "common to man" — **ἀνθρώπινος** (*anthropinos*): anything experienced by human beings; unexceptional; merely human

4. "but God is faithful" — **πιστὸς δὲ ὁ Θεός** (*pistos de ho Theos*): but God is categorically faithful

5. "suffer" — **ἐάω** (*eao*): to permit, such as a lurking danger

6. "above" — **ὑπὲρ** (*huper*): over, above, beyond; more than; beyond what is normal; something that is excessive

7. "able" — **δύναμαι** (*dunamai*): depicts strength that makes one able, capable, strong, and powerful

8. "with" — **σύν** (*sun*): with; together with; alongside with; accompanying

9. "make" — **ποιέω** (*poieo*): make; creatively make; manufacture or produce; to provide

10. "escape" — **ἔκβασις** (*ekbasis*): to walk out, as to walk out of a difficult place; to walk away; to remove yourself from a person or place that isn't good for you; to use your feet to exit a situation or environment

11. "bear" — **ὑποφέρω** (*hupophero*): from **ὑπό** (*hupo*) and **φέρω** (*phero*); the word **ὑπό** (*hupo*) means under and the word **φέρω** (*phero*) means

to bear or to carry on; technically, like an undercurrent of a river that sweeps or carries one away; to be carried safely away from danger

12. "flee" — φεύγω (*pheugo*): to run as fast as possible; to escape; to use one's feet to move as fast as possible to get out of an unprofitable situation; picture of one's feet "flying" as he runs from a situation

13. "youthful" — νεωτερικός (*neoterikos*): youthful, immature; juvenile

14. "lusts" — ἐπιθυμία (*epithumia*): compound of ἐπί (*epi*) and θυμός (*thumos*); the word ἐπί (*epi*) means over and is used as an intensifier; the word θυμός (*thumos*) depicts heated passions; compounded, it is intense heated passions or intense passionate desire

15. "possess" — κτάομαι (*ktaomai*): to control; to manage; to possess; or to win the mastery over

16. "vessel" — σκεῦος (*skeuos*): describes the human body as a vessel to contain something; depicts a household utensil or any instrument by which anything is done

17. "sanctification" — ἁγιασμός (*hagiasmos*): complete separation; holy in practice; from ἅγιος (*hagios*), which describes something that is set apart; consecrated; holy

18. "honor" — τιμή (*time*): valuable; of great worth; or honorable

19. "provision" — πρόνοια (*pronoia*): compound of πρό (*pro*) and νοέω (*noeo*); the word πρό (*pro*) means in advance and νοέω (*noeo*) means to think; forethought; to think through in advance; hence, advanced planning

20. "marriage" — γάμος (*gamos*): marriage; holy matrimony

21. "marriage bed" — κοίτη (*koite*): sexual intercourse between a husband and wife

22. "undefiled" — ἀμίαντος (*amiantos*): free from blemish, especially moral blemish

23. "sexually immoral" — πόρνος (*pornos*): any type of sex with another person outside the bond of marriage, includes sexual activity by non-married individuals, including both adultery and homosexuality; the word for prostitution or love that is sold for money

24. "adulterous" — μοιχός (*moichos*): one who violates another; to take something illegally; to seduce another person's spouse; one who violates a marital commitment by having a sexual relationship outside the covenant of marriage; a seducer; one who is guilty of indecent sexual behavior

25. "fault" — **παράπτωμα** (*paraptoma*): a falling in some area of one's life; to transgress; to misstep; to lapse; could be an actual falling into sin, or a tripping in the way one thinks or how he behaves; a person who has fallen, failed, erred, or made some kind of mistake; may denote a person who has accidentally swerved, turned amiss, or one who has done something knowingly wrong; hence, a transgression or trespass

## SYNOPSIS

The temple of Apollo, located in the ancient city of Hierapolis, was a pagan temple where pagan gods were worshiped. Hierapolis, a large military city, was positioned not far from the city of Laodicea, which was the financial center of the whole valley where these cities were situated. And not far from Laodicea was the sleepy little town called Colossae, a place where people went for recreation and relaxation because of the cool refreshing waters that came down from the mountains.

These cities were filled with pagan deities, and they were also filled with people who were making critical mistakes with both their faith, and their morals. Drunkenness and sexual debauchery were common in these cities. They had not been taught the Bible, so they had no Scriptural foundation for their lives. They made all kinds of critical miscalculations — both morally and ethically. They didn't know how to be husbands and wives, or fathers and mothers. They had no idea of how to work properly, or if it was right or wrong to do things like steal or commit adultery.

These seem like very basic things to us, but in a world where there was no Bible, people had to figure things out on their own. And consequently, they made mistakes. Unfortunately, that's the same problem people are confronting in society today — at the end of the age — because the presence of the Bible has been so diminished in society. Many people grow up — and just like the pagans of the past — they don't know what the Bible teaches about elementary things like morals, ethics, and what is right or wrong. People today are even confused about their gender.

The Bible makes all these things clear, and we have a responsibility to bring the teaching of the Bible to people, and to give them a good, solid foundation — especially since we are living in the end of the age.

**The emphasis of this lesson:**

You have the power of the Holy Spirit on the inside, and you do not have to yield to *any* form of temptation. God will give you wisdom to divert sexual temptation, or if it has already tried to grip you, know that the Holy Spirit lives in you and He will help you overcome it. In this lesson you will be equipped to obey the Bible and use your feet to *flee* from sexual temptation.

# A Final Review of Our Anchor Verse

"There hath no temptation taken you but such as is common to man: but God is faithful, who will not suffer you to be tempted above that ye are able; but will with the temptation also make a way to escape, that ye may be able to bear it" (1 Corinthians 10:13). The word "temptation" — the Greek word *peirasmos* — describes a fiery trial intended to destroy.

The word "taken" is a form of the Greek word *lambano*, which means *to seize; to attack; to grip; to take hold of.* Here we see the lure of the flesh to grab hold of you, seduce you, and drag you into some kind of inappropriate action. There has no temptation taken you but such as is "common to man." The phrase "common to man" is from the Greek word *anthropinos*, which describes *anything experienced by all human beings; unexceptional;* and *merely human.* When the flesh calls out to you, you don't have to fear and tremble. Instead, look at temptation and say, "You are nothing! Other people have faced you and conquered you, and I will too!" There's nothing exceptional about it, so diminish it! Don't magnify temptation and give power to it. Diminish it, and it will be easier to overcome.

The verse goes on to say, "...But God is faithful, who will not suffer you to be tempted above that ye are able...." The word "able," a form of the Greek word *dunamai*, describes *strength that makes one able, strong, and powerful.* It means that by the power of the Holy Spirit God has given you the ability to *master* this temptation.

# Your Way of Escape Is in Your Shoes

First Corinthians 10:13 goes on to say, "But will with the temptation also make a way to escape...." The word "with" — the Greek word *sun* — carries the idea of partnership and cooperation. When our faithful God sees that we're in a difficult place, He is right there with us as our partner. He is cooperating *with* us to make a way of escape.

The word "make" — the Greek word *poieo* — means to *make; creatively make;* to *manufacture or produce;* and *to provide*. God will provide a way of escape. If He has to, He'll create or manufacture a way out. That is how much He wants you to remain free! The word "escape," the Greek word *ekbasis,* is from the word *ek* which means *out* — where we get the word "exit" — and the word *basis* which means *to step*. But when you compound the two words to form *ekbasis* — the word translated as "escape" — it literally means *to walk out; to walk away; to remove yourself from a person or place that isn't good for you;* and *to use your feet to exit a situation or environment.*

If you find yourself in a place where you're sexually tempted, don't stay there and say, "I'm going to stay here until I overcome." That is foolish! The Bible says your way of escape is in your shoes. It's called *your feet*. Just like you walked *into* a bad situation, you need to make a decision to let God partner with you so you can turn around and walk *out* of that situation.

First Corinthians 10:13 concludes, "That ye may be able to bear it." The word "bear" is the Greek word *hupophero*. And *hupo* means *under,* while the word *phero* means *to bear or to carry;* but when you put the two words together it pictures *an undertow or an undercurrent that takes you out of a turbulent situation and delivers you safely away from danger.* If you'll cooperate with the grace of God, it will take you *out* of that temptation and will swiftly deposit you far from it in a place where you are delivered, safe, and free.

## Flee From Sexual Temptation

Sexual temptations were common with the Corinthians, so the apostle Paul wrote in the very next verse, "Wherefore, my dearly beloved, flee from idolatry" (1 Corinthians 10:14). Idolatrous places were places of sexual immorality, all kinds of sexual debauchery, and promiscuity. All of that occurred in places of idolatry, so when Paul said, "flee" from idolatry, he was literally saying, "Flee from sexual temptation."

In order to "flee," you need to use your feet to get out of there. The word "flee" in Greek means *to run as fast as possible*. It depicts *escaping a situation;* and *using one's feet to move as fast as possible to get out of an unprofitable situation.* It pictures *one's feet "flying" as he runs from something.* In other words, "If you're in a place where you're about to yield to temptation, move your feet; let your feet fly as you escape from that situation." It's smart to run from temptation!

We've already seen that we can divert and overcome emotionally upsetting temptations. We've learned how to overcome overeating temptations, and we've discovered God has given us the power to overcome overspending temptations. In this lesson, we're focusing on overcoming sexual temptations.

# 'Flee Also Youthful Lusts'

When you sin sexually, you violate the Holy Spirit who lives on the inside of you, and that is the greatest offense of all. The Greater One lives in you, and He is the Spirit of Holiness. When you sexually sin, you drag Him into that act of sin. It violates the Holy Spirit. Not only that, but it violates others. You end up living with regret and in personal defeat. You end up living in sin. This is why the apostle Paul wrote, "Flee also youthful lusts..." (2 Timothy 2:22).

Notice the word "flee" again — which means *to run as fast as possible*; and *to escape*. It pictures *one's feet flying as he runs from a situation*. In Second Timothy 2:22, when Paul said, "Flee also youthful lusts..." he literally meant, "Hit the trail and run as fast as you can." The word "youthful" depicts *youthful, immature,* or *juvenile* lusts — which means it is juvenile to commit sexual sin. It is *immature* in the mind of God.

The word "lusts" is the Greek word *epithumia*, a compound of *epi* and *thumos*. The word *epi* means *over* and *is used as an intensifier*. The word *thumos* depicts *heated passions*. Compounded, *epithumia* means *intense heated passions* or *intense passionate desire*. This describes when the flesh reaches out to seize you, and you feel like you just can't say "no." It's heated, passionate, and *juvenile*. The way you overcome this temptation is to use your feet. Run from that place — get out of there as fast as you can!

# Possess Your Vessel in Sanctification and Honor

In First Thessalonians 4:4, Paul refers to our bodies and how we're to manage temptations: "That every one of you should know how to possess his vessel in sanctification and honour." He's talking about the human body, and that we should know how to "possess" it. The word "possess," the Greek word *ktaomai*, means *to control*, so you could translate it, "We should know how to *control* our bodies." *Ktaomai* also means *to manage*, and therefore could be translated, "We should know how to *manage* our bodies." It means *to win the mastery over* — hence, "We should know how to *win the mastery over* our bodies."

In this particular case, the body is called a "vessel" — the Greek word *skeuos* — which *describes the human body as a vessel to contain something*. The verse says every one of us should know how to possess his own "vessel." We are vessels for the Holy Spirit. We are instruments to be used for the glory of God. And when we surrender our bodies to be used in another way, it is a violation. That is why Paul said we need to know how to possess our vessels "in sanctification and honor."

The word "sanctification" — the Greek word *hagiasmos* — means *complete separation*; and *holy in practice*. It is from the Greek word *hagios*, which describes *something that is set apart*; *consecrated*; and *holy*. It tells us our bodies do not belong to us — our bodies belong to the Lord. When we committed ourselves to Christ, He *separated* us, *sanctified* us, and *consecrated* us. And the Bible says your body should be held in "honor." The word "honor" is the Greek word *time*, which means *of great worth*; and *valuable*.

## You Are a Walking Sanctuary of His Presence

In God's eyes, your body is valuable, precious, and the dwelling place of the Holy Spirit. That is why Paul told us in Romans 13:14 (*ESV*), "But put on the Lord Jesus Christ, and make no provision for the flesh, to gratify its desires."

The word "provision" — the Greek word *pronoia* — is a compound of two words. The word *pro* means *in advance*, and *noeo* means *to think*. When you compound the words *pro* and *noeo*, it forms the word *pronoia*, which describes *forethought*; *to think through in advance*; hence, *advanced planning*. In this verse Paul said, "Don't do it! Don't do it! Don't do it! *Do not* make plans for your flesh to gratify its desires!" The word "gratify" means *to satisfy* or *provide for its lusts*. My friend, we are *not* to do that. We are the temple of the Holy Spirit, and we're to honor the fact that His presence lives within us.

"Let marriage be held in honor among all, and let the marriage bed be undefiled, for God will judge the sexually immoral and adulterous" (Hebrews 13:4 *ESV*). The word "marriage" in this verse is the word *gamos*, and refers to a monogamous *marriage*; or *holy matrimony*. The word "marriage bed" — the Greek word *koite* — refers to *sexual intercourse between a husband and wife*. And the word "undefiled" means *free from blemish*; especially *moral blemish*. In other words, "God wants us to treat the marriage bed like it is holy; it is to be free from all sexual blemish." Paul adds, "…For God will judge the sexually immoral and the adulterous" (Hebrews 13:4 *ESV*).

The Greek word for "sexually immoral" is *pornos*, and it describes *any type of sex with another person outside the bond of marriage*. It involves *sexual activity by non-married individuals, including both adultery and homosexuality*. The word "adulterous" is the Greek word *moichos*, which describes *one who violates another; to take something illegally; to seduce another person's spouse; one who violates a marital commitment by having a sexual relationship outside the covenant of marriage*; and *a seducer*.

The Bible says God judges those things, and we are not to ever go in that direction. If you feel tempted, then you need to use your feet. Put space between you and that other person. Create space between you and pornography. Add a filter on your computer that identifies to someone else if you looked at something you shouldn't look at. Accountability will help you not to yield to temptation. Put up a barricade; build some kind of a border so that you put space between yourself and those things that are wrong.

## If You Have Fallen Into Sin, There Is Restoration

If you know someone who has fallen into sin, *restore* them. "Brethren, if a man be overtaken in a fault, ye which are spiritual, restore such an one in the spirit of meekness; considering thyself, lest thou also be tempted" (Galatians 6:1). The word "fault" — the Greek word *paraptoma*, describes *a falling in some area of one's life; to transgress; to misstep; to lapse; it could be an actual falling into sin*; or *a tripping in the way one thinks, or how he behaves*. It depicts *a person who has fallen, failed, erred, or made some kind of mistake*. It may denote *a person who has accidentally swerved, turned amiss, or one who has done something knowingly wrong*; hence, *a transgression or trespass*.

If a person is sorry and has a repentant heart, they are to be forgiven. And we who are partnering with God are to do what we can to help *restore* that individual. Judgment and condemnation are never a blessing; they never help. Remember, you reap what you sow (*see* Galatians 6:7). If you know someone who has fallen into sin, and you sow judgment and condemnation, that is what you will reap. Choose instead to take the position of mercy, and help *restore* the person who has fallen. But if you're the person being tempted, then obey First Corinthians 10:13, and use your feet to flee from the temptation! With the help of the Holy Spirit within, you *can have victory* over sexual temptation!

## STUDY QUESTIONS

Study to shew thyself approved unto God, a workman that needeth
not to be ashamed, rightly dividing the word of truth.
— 2 Timothy 2:15

1.  God has good plans for your life (*see* Jeremiah 29:11-13 and Ephesians 2:10). When temptation comes, it tries to stop God's good plans from coming to pass in your life. Notice how Joseph was tempted, he ran from the temptation and fulfilled his destiny (*see* Genesis 39:7-12). In contrast, Samson laid down in the lap of temptation (*see* Judges 16:15-21). What happened to Samson as a result? What type of consequences may occur for yielding to sexual temptation? Can the consequences of sexual sin reach far beyond the heat of the moment?
2.  Consider First Corinthians 6:18-20 and Second Corinthians 6:16,17. In God's eyes, your body is something precious and exceedingly valuable. If God sees your body as valuable, shouldn't *you*? You are His home; the Holy Spirit lives within you. Why is it important to learn to control your body?
3.  According to First Peter 2:11 and First Thessalonians 5:22, what are two things we are instructed to abstain from? Why are we to abstain from them? Practically speaking, how can we do that? How can obeying these verses help you divert sexual temptation?

## PRACTICAL APPLICATION

But be ye doers of the word, and not hearers only,
deceiving your own selves.
— James 1:22

1.  You have to get very practical about diverting and overcoming sexual temptation. What type of barricade can you surround yourself with to create space between you and things that are wrong? Write down the names of the *people* you need space from in order to avoid sexual temptation. Write down the *places* you need to avoid to divert sexual temptation. Write out a plan of action and ask someone to hold you

accountable to it. Pray over your plan and ask the Holy Spirit to help you execute it.

2. Make a covenant with your eyes, and choose to walk in purity.

   • "I made a covenant with mine eyes; why then should I think upon a maid" (Job 31:1).

   • "Turn away my eyes from looking at worthless things, *and* revive me in Your way" (Psalm 119:37 *NKJV*).

   • "I will set no wicked thing before mine eyes..." (Psalm 101:3).

3. If you yielded to temptation and you repented, there is restoration for you (*see* 1 John 1:9 and 2 Corinthians 5:17). Keep in mind that knowing God will forgive you isn't a pass to yield to temptation in the future. Ask Him for strength to resist temptation when it arises (*see* Psalm 119:11 and 2 Corinthians 10:5). Consecrate yourself in a fresh new way to the Lord, and commit yourself wholly to Him. "I have refrained my feet from every evil way, that I might keep thy word" (Psalm 119:101).

# Notes

_____

_____

_____

_____

_____

_____

_____

_____

_____

_____

_____

_____

_____

_____

_____

_____

_____

_____

_____

_____

_____

_____

_____

_____

_____

_____

_____

_____

_____

_____

_____

# Notes

_____
_____
_____
_____
_____
_____
_____
_____
_____
_____
_____
_____
_____
_____
_____
_____
_____
_____
_____
_____
_____
_____
_____
_____
_____
_____
_____

www.ingramcontent.com/pod-product-compliance
Lightning Source LLC
Chambersburg PA
CBHW051048030426
42339CB00006B/249